An Essay on "A Book of Five rings" by Miyamoto Musashi

By John Mortimer

(21st August 1994)

An Essay on "A Book of Five Rings" by Miyamoto Musashi.

Copyrighted Material

An Essay on a Book of Five Rings by Miyamoto Musashi

ISBN 10:1511758503

ISBN 13: 9781511758505

Copyright © John R Mortimer 2014

Published by Smashwords

"A Book of Five Rings" was written in 1645 by Miyamoto Musashi, a renowned Japanese swordsman. It was written shortly before his death while living in seclusion in a cave in the mountains of Kyushu. He was born in 1584 to the Samurai class. Japan at that time was unstable politically. The Shogun had taken control and the ordinary Samurai, who were not Lords and had no lands, had no way of making a living now that the wars between the clans were over. He became a "Ronin" after fighting in different wars and having many duels wherein he remained undefeated. He earned respect as a great swordsman of his time. Later in life, after many years of fighting, he worked at other disciplines, such as painting and sculpture, in order to broaden his knowledge. From what he says in his book "A Book of Five Rings" we know he had his own school of swordsmanship and in the time just before his death he wanted to pass on to future generations some of his skills by writing his ideas down. It is still used today, not only in Japan but worldwide, for use in many situations in modern life. Musashi starts his "Book of Five Rings" with an introduction. This describes fighting life and the fact that he had natural ability and the other schools were inferior. He also tells us how he broadened his mind and abilities by being self-taught in many arts and disciplines.

The Ground Book

The first chapter of "The Book of Five Rings" is called the Ground Book. Musashi tells us that this book is the way of strategy and is the craft of the warrior. He tells us that the warrior should also be an artist and not stick exclusively to training as a warrior, as he himself found later in life. He also says that a warrior must have a "resolute acceptance of death". Strategy is defined as the art of planning and directing. He goes on to say that his contemporaries are not true strategists and that in the old days it was beneficial practice to many arts, not just Sword fighting. He was very insistent that the ground work of the art is correct before using flashy techniques for profit. These do not work. He categorises the four different lifestyles of men in his lifetime. They are gentlemen, farmers, artisans and merchants and all have their own arts and strategies so they are able to succeed. He shows us a comparison between the way of carpentry and the way of the warrior, showing how familiar each craft's strategy is to the other.

Next, he describes what each of the books stand for. For the Ground Book, he says "know the smallest and the biggest, the shallowest things and the deepest." ALL is important. Water is the basis of the second book. The spirit becomes the water from a single drop of water to the sea. The Fire book tells us about fighting and combat. The fire burns differently as the conditions, seen or unseen, develop. The Wind Book is the book of tradition and we are told to stay on the correct path without wandering off it. The Void is the final book, the emptying of the full receptacle so that each movement comes without thought. He goes on to describe the basis of his own school. He teaches the use of the two swords but this is only the use of that which is carried naturally or under normal circumstances. He knows that weapons have their place, but to him, the sword is the true and only weapon, the extension of his own being, not only his body. He follows the way utterly without following other ideas or beliefs.

He describes the different kinds of weapons and their uses stressing that they should be of good quality. Different weapons have different uses depending on different conditions and the distance of your opponent. The gun is the ultimate weapon but only from a distance, in those days close-up fighting was done with a sword. A warrior should be familiar with all weapons and not stick to practising with one and not the others because sometimes a different strategy is needed. Timing is very important and can only come with practice. Timing and rhythm are necessary in all aspects of the warrior's art even in the void. Timing is also important to other disciplines to be sure of success.

He summarises his strategy by the following nine points.

Do not think dishonestly.
The way is in training.
Become acquainted with every art.
Know the ways of all professions
Distinguish between gain and loss in worldly matters.
Develop intuitive judgement and understanding for everything.
Perceive those things that cannot be seen.
Pay attention even to trifles.
Do nothing which is of no use.

To become the superior man he demonstrates how to become a master by sticking to the way and by practising night and day to achieve his ends.

The Water Book

The second chapter is called the Water Book, the book of spirit. Musashi stresses that if the book is not understood properly, the way will be lost. Although it is written for single combat it can be expanded to any number. Your spirit must be the same whether in fighting or in normal day to day circumstances. Although you must be calm you should be alert at all times. If you are tired do not let your spirit follow. You must maintain a constant level at all times. Stance is important and must be maintained under all conditions. Gaze is an extension of your stance and you must take in all around you, not just the small part directly in front. Don't be distracted by any slight movement. The sword should be held firmly but not tense and not loose. The same grip must be maintained whether holding or cutting with the sword. The feet must move as in walking no matter the speed or length of step. Both feet should be used equally. Attitude must be natural whatever happens. No matter which way you move the cut must be made. You must wield the long sword naturally and cutting firmly and return. But his can only be achieved by constant practice.

The tactics used are always let the enemy attack first and counter the move, never going back, you must be able to adjust to the opponents attack and be able to engage and react without having to think about it. Lull your opponent into a false sense of security and follow up. When your attack comes simultaneously, having no fear and not letting your opponent know from where your attack is coming will give you an advantage. It is important that all the different methods of attack are practiced constantly until they happen without thought for your own self.

Interestingly, however, although his school was of the Two Swords Style, when up against another skilful swordsman he only used one weapon. He used the words "Two Swords" not literally. He meant use all one's ingenuity in combat.

Schools can only give you the basis but it comes back to each individual to achieve a good development of his mind and body to work as one without thought first. This will only come with constant practice, never losing the importance of the basic moves.

The Fire Book

Again, in Keeping with his use of the basic elements, he calls his third chapter the Fire Book. The book is about fighting, the ferocity of fighting, fierce like the flame. Try always to attain a higher position with the sun to your right. In a building, the entrance must be behind you or to the right. At night the light from the fire should be behind so that the opponent can only see you in silhouette. Chase the enemy into difficult positions so that he cannot move freely.

He states that there are three methods to forestall the enemy. The first "Ken No Sen" which means to "set him up". The second is "Tan No Sen" which is to wait for the initiative and the last is called "Tai No Sen" to accompany and forestall him. In all cases you must remain calm and be decisive in whatever you do, maintaining a strong spirit and adapting to whatever happens. You must supress the enemy's techniques and attack at his weak points so that you command the situation. It is necessary to understand when your opponent might have his spirit lowered or may be about to change his position or his own strategy and use this to your advantage. He says that we must be prepared for battle before the enemy can attack us and not be caught preparing our weapons. Our attack must come while the enemy is still using long-distance tactics, we must go in with short-distance tactics before they are ready to change. This is the essence of forestalling the enemy. When the opponent wanes, you must take every advantage, if you do not keep the pressure on, the opponent may come back the stronger. You must understand your opponent's position but don't give away any thought to what his abilities may be.

To gain ascendancy in an equal situation you must change your tactics to gain the element of surprise. To discover his abilities you must draw him out. You must extend a false spirit and when the moment shows, extend your true spirit not giving him a chance to regain his. You can frighten your opposition by the use of noise, weapons or stature. In battle as in single combat by injuring the extremities you can defeat the whole. Confuse your opposition by never letting him understand your way. The voice is a weapon used to distract and frighten. It is very important to use it in different ways for different occasions. When fighting, direct the ferocity of the attack to his strengths which will give you complete victory. You must crush the opponent totally. When you have the advantage never let him recover. You must vary his tactics, not to repeat any failures a second time which will expose you to defeat. You must defeat your enemy to the core of his being. If he is not totally crushed he can revive. We must look at the whole, not just the small points. The enemy should be moved by your own will, unable to move under his own volition. If the opponent is intimidated sufficiently you may be able to win without resorting to fighting. You must follow the way without fear of the consequences.

The Wind Book

The Wind Book is the fourth chapter of "A Book of Five Rings". In this book, Musashi appears to be merely comparing schools, but it really goes deeper than that. We need to know the ways of other teachings so that we can, by understanding their ways, defeat them. He discusses tactics in relation to the use of the extra Long-sword and its problems of always needing space to fight in. Strong or weak has no place for the true spirit, meaning if you rely on strength alone, it's not enough, you may be course in your movements. Using a shorter Long-sword is also not the way to win. It appears to be easier to handle, but relying on jumping in close to jab will not always defeat someone who follows the true way. Many schools blind beginners by the use of flashy techniques to sell their way. By standing tall and straight (natural) and causing the opponent to twist and bend you have the advantage. He stresses that when duelling, it is the intention to take the lead and frustrate his rhythm as much as possible. Other schools teach specific places to look at. Musashi disagrees. He says that you should see all. You must not use unnatural movements, your feet should be firmly on the ground and the feet should always move in a normal walking motion. If they are too rushed, or too slow, this will be to your disadvantage.

The Book of the Void

He ends this book with some very important points. Pupils must only be taught according to their ability to understand. If they are taught too much, too soon they will become muddled and the way will be lost. As Musashi says "The method of teaching my strategy is with a trustworthy spirit. You must train diligently." Musashi finishes his teaching with The Book of the Void. He says "of course the void is nothingness". But to understand this, your knowledge needs to be great and continually expanding. You need to empty the full vessel. His last words describe his total beliefs. "In the Void is virtue and no evil. Wisdom had existence, principle has existence, and spirit is nothingness."

In summary, we cannot always be the void. Now we must be the gentleman, the farmer, the artisan and the merchant to live in our own time and survive. It is probable that the likes of Musashi will not be seen again unless we can live a simpler life in another time.

Printed in Great Britain
by Amazon